HOMEMADE HEALTHY DOG FOOD COOKBOOK

Mouthwatering Recipes To Cook Nutritious Meals For Your Furry Friend

Carissa Vincent

Table of Contents

Introduction..4

Chapter 1...6

    Why Homemade Dog Food...6

    The Importance Of Homemade Dog Food..........................7

    Understanding Dog Nutrition...8

Chapter 2...11

    Ingredients And Equipment...11

    Essential Ingredients For Homemade Dog Food...............11

    Recommended Kitchen Equipment...................................12

Chapter 3...15

    What Your Dog Should Eat..15

    The Amount Of Food That Your Dog Should Be Fed........17

Chapter 4...20

    Mouth-Watering Homemade Meals For Your Dog...........20

Chapter 5...58

    Treats..58

Chapter 6...68

    Snacks...68

Chapter 7...80

Special Diets 80

Grain-Free Recipes 80

Raw Food 87

Chapter 8 94

Storage and Serving of Homemade Dog Food 94

Storing Homemade Dog Food 94

Serving Homemade Dog Food 95

Chapter 9 98

Health and Wellness 98

Tips for maintaining a healthy dog 98

Common Diseases in Dogs and How To Treat Them
Naturally 100

Conclusion 103

Introduction

As pet owners, we all want to ensure that our furry friends are receiving the best possible nutrition. One of the best ways to do this is by preparing homemade meals for our dogs. In this cookbook, you'll find a variety of recipes that are not only delicious and nutritious for your dog, but also easy to make.

Homemade dog food has become increasingly popular in recent years as pet owners have become more aware of the importance of high-quality, nutritious food for their dogs. By preparing homemade meals, you have complete control over the ingredients, ensuring that you know exactly what your dog is eating.

This can be especially important for dogs with food sensitivities or allergies. Additionally, homemade dog food is often less expensive than commercial brands and can be tailored to your dog's specific needs.

Before you begin preparing homemade meals for your dog, it's important to understand some basic safety precautions. Consult with your veterinarian to ensure that your dog's diet is nutritionally balanced and appropriate for its individual needs. It's also important to be aware of foods that are toxic to dogs, such as chocolate, grapes, and onions. Be sure to store and handle ingredients safely to prevent contamination and food-borne illnesses.

In this cookbook, you'll find a wide range of recipes for dogs of all ages, sizes, and dietary needs. From basic recipes such as chicken and rice to more advanced recipes like lamb and brown rice, there's something for every dog. We also include recipes for specialty diets, such as grain-free. For those who are looking for a special treat, we have a variety of recipes for homemade dog biscuits and snacks.

In addition to recipes, we also provide additional resources and a glossary of terms to help you navigate the world of homemade dog food. From equipment and ingredients to nutritional information, this cookbook is your comprehensive guide to preparing healthy, delicious meals for your furry friend.

So, whether you're a seasoned cook or new to the kitchen, our recipes will guide you through the process of making healthy, delicious meals for your dog.

Chapter 1

Why Homemade Dog Food

Homemade dog food has become increasingly popular in recent years as pet owners have become more aware of the importance of high-quality, nutritious food for their dogs. There are several reasons why many pet owners choose to make homemade dog food:

1. **Control over ingredients:** By preparing homemade meals, you have complete control over the ingredients, ensuring that you know exactly what your dog is eating. This can be especially important for dogs with food sensitivities or allergies.

2. **Tailored to specific needs:** Homemade dog

food can be tailored to your dog's specific needs, such as age, size, and activity level. You can also adjust the recipes to suit your dog's preferences.

3. **Cost-effective:** Homemade dog food is often less expensive than commercial brands. By buying ingredients in bulk and preparing meals at home, you can save money in the long run.

4. **Better quality:** Homemade dog food is often made with fresher and higher-quality ingredients than commercial brands. This can lead to improved health and well-being for your dog.

5. **Reduce packaging waste:** Homemade dog food also helps to reduce packaging waste and be more environmentally friendly.

The Importance Of Homemade Dog Food

Homemade dog food is an important option for pet

owners who want to ensure that their dogs are receiving the best possible nutrition. Here are a few reasons why homemade dog food is important:

- **Nutritional balance:** You can ensure that your dog's diet is nutritionally balanced with homemade food, by adding all the vitamins and minerals your dog needs to stay healthy.

- **Increased variety:** Homemade dog food allows you to offer your dog a variety of flavors and textures, which can help keep them interested in their food.

- **Reduce packaging waste:** Homemade dog food also helps to reduce packaging waste and be more environmentally friendly.

- **Bonding:** Preparing homemade dog food can be a fun and rewarding experience for both you and your dog. It can also be a way to bond with your dog and show them how much you care about their health and well-being.

- **Quality control:** Preparing homemade dog food allows pet owners to control the quality of the ingredients used and ensure that their dog is getting the best possible nutrition.

- **Reduced risk of contamination:** Homemade dog food reduces the risk of contamination from unhealthy preservatives and chemicals found in commercial dog food.

Understanding Dog Nutrition

Understanding dog nutrition is essential for ensuring that your furry friend is receiving the best possible diet. Here are a few key factors to consider when understanding dog nutrition:

- **Protein:** Dogs require a diet that is high in protein, as it is essential for maintaining healthy muscles, bones, and skin. Meat, fish, and eggs are good sources of protein.

- **Fats:** Fats are an important part of a dog's diet, as they provide energy and help to absorb certain vitamins and minerals. Omega-3 and omega-6 unsaturated fats are significant for keeping a sound coat and skin.

- **Carbohydrates:** Carbohydrates provide energy for dogs and are found in grains such as rice, wheat, and barley.

- **Vitamins and minerals:** Vitamins and minerals are essential for maintaining a dog's overall health. Some important vitamins and minerals for dogs include calcium, phosphorus, and vitamin D for healthy bones, and vitamins A, E, and C for healthy skin, eyes, and immune systems.

- **Water:** Water is essential for maintaining a dog's health, and dogs should have access to fresh, clean water at all times.

- **Age, size, and activity level:** The nutritional needs of a dog will vary depending on its age, size, and activity level. Puppies, for example, have different nutritional needs than adult dogs, and smaller breeds have different needs than larger breeds.

It's essential to consult with a veterinarian to determine your dog's specific nutritional needs and to feed them a balanced diet that meets those needs. Homemade dog food can be a great option as it allows you to control the ingredients and tailor the diet to your dog's specific needs, but it's important to ensure that the diet is nutritionally balanced and appropriate for your dog.

Chapter 2

Ingredients And Equipment

Essential Ingredients For Homemade Dog Food

There are several essential ingredients that you should include when preparing homemade dog food:

- **Protein:** Meat, fish, and eggs are good sources of protein for dogs. Some examples include chicken, beef, fish, turkey, and lamb.

- **Vegetables:** Vegetables such as carrots, green beans, broccoli, and spinach provide essential vitamins and minerals for dogs.

- **Carbohydrates:** Grains such as rice, barley, and oats provide carbohydrates for energy and can be used as a base for dog food.

- **Fats:** Fats such as olive oil, coconut oil, and flaxseed oil provide energy and help to absorb certain vitamins and minerals.

- **Supplements:** A balanced diet for dogs should also contain vitamins and minerals, such as calcium, phosphorus, and vitamin D for healthy bones, and vitamins A, E, and C for healthy skin, eyes, and immune systems.

- **Water:** Water is essential for maintaining a dog's health, and dogs should have access to fresh, clean water at all times.

It's important to consult with a veterinarian to determine your dog's specific nutritional needs and to use appropriate ingredients that meet those needs.

Recommended Kitchen Equipment

Here are some recommended kitchen equipment for preparing homemade dog food:

- **Cutting board:** A sturdy cutting board is essential for chopping and dicing ingredients.

- **Knife set:** A good quality knife set will make it easier to chop and dice ingredients.

- **Measuring cups and spoons:** Accurate measuring is important when preparing homemade dog food, so measuring cups and spoons is essential.

- **Mixing bowls:** Mixing bowls are essential for combining ingredients and making treats

- **Pot or pan:** A pot or pan is necessary for cooking and heating ingredients.

- **Slow cooker:** Slow cookers are great for making large batches of dog food that can be stored in the freezer.

- **Blender or food processor:** A blender or food processor can be used to grind or puree ingredients.

- **Silicone ice cube trays:** Silicone ice cube trays are perfect for making small portions of dog food that can be stored in the freezer.

- **Tongs:** tongs are useful for handling hot ingredients or for picking up meat from a slow cooker.

- Strainer: A strainer is useful for draining and rinsing grains, vegetables, and fruits.

It's important to keep in mind that not all equipment may be necessary and it also depends on the type of recipes you want to prepare for your dog.

Chapter 3

What Your Dog Should Eat

There are certain foods that should be avoided by dogs, as they can be toxic and potentially harmful to their health. Here is a list of some common foods that should be avoided or should be fed with caution to your dogs. They include:

1. **Chocolate:** Chocolate contains a compound called theobromine, which can be harmful to canines. Dark chocolate and unsweetened baking chocolate have higher levels of theobromine and are more dangerous than milk chocolate.

2. **Grapes and raisins:** Grapes and raisins can cause kidney disappointment in canines, even in limited quantities.

3. **Onions and garlic:** Onions and garlic contain compounds that can harm canines' red platelets, prompting anemia.

4. **Alcohol:** Alcohol can cause vomiting, diarrhea, and even coma or death in dogs.

5. **Avocados:** Avocados contain persin, which can cause retching and diarrhea in canines. They can be fed to your dogs in very small quantities or not at all, it depends on your preference.

6. **Coffee, tea, and other caffeinated drinks:** Caffeine can be toxic to dogs and can cause restlessness, rapid breathing, heart palpitations, muscle tremors, and even seizures.

7. **Nuts:** Some nuts such as macadamia nuts and walnuts can cause vomiting, diarrhea, and even pancreatitis in dogs.

8. **Fatty foods:** Foods high in fat such as bacon or sausage can cause pancreatitis in dogs.

9. **Bones:** Bones can splinter and cause blockages or perforations in a dog's digestive tract. This may not be avoided as they can be fed to your dog. But it is essential that you keep an eye on the dog whilst your dog eats

the bone.

10. **Dairy products:** Some dogs may be lactose intolerant, so it's important to avoid giving them dairy products such as milk, cheese, and ice cream.

It's important to keep in mind that this list is not exhaustive and there are other foods that may be harmful to dogs. If you suspect your dog has ingested something toxic, contact your veterinarian immediately.

The Amount Of Food That Your Dog Should Be Fed

The amount of food that you should feed different dogs will depend on several factors such as their age, size, breed, and activity level. Here are some guidelines for feeding different types of dogs:

- **Puppies:** Puppies have different nutritional needs than adult dogs, and they require more calories per pound of body weight than adult dogs. They also need to eat more frequently, usually three to four small meals per day. Puppies should be fed a diet that is high in protein and fat, and that includes all the necessary vitamins and minerals for growth and development.

- **Adult dogs:** Adult dogs require fewer calories per pound of body weight than puppies, and they can usually eat two meals per day. Adult dogs should be fed a diet that is balanced and includes all the necessary vitamins and minerals for the maintenance of overall health.

- **Senior dogs:** As dogs age, their metabolism slows down, and they typically require fewer calories. They may also have dental issues that make it difficult for them to eat solid food, so you may need to offer them softer food options. Senior dogs should be fed a diet that is easy to digest and that includes all the necessary vitamins and minerals for maintaining overall health.

- **Working dogs:** Dogs that are used for working purposes such as hunting, herding, and agility training require more calories than sedentary dogs. They also need a diet that is high in protein and fat for energy and endurance.

- Dogs with special needs: Dogs with certain health conditions such as diabetes, kidney disease, or food allergies, require a specialized diet that is tailored to their specific needs. Consult with a veterinarian to determine the appropriate diet for your dog.

Chapter 4

Mouth-Watering Homemade Meals For Your Dog

Egg and Vegetable Omelet:

Ingredients:

2 eggs

1/4 cup diced vegetables (carrots, green beans, and broccoli)

1 tablespoon olive oil.

Instructions:

Whisk together eggs in a bowl.

Heat olive oil in a pan over medium heat, add diced vegetables, and cook for a few minutes.

Eggs should be cooked until set after being poured over veggies.

Cut into small pieces and serve.

Calories: approximately 150-200 calories per serving.

Amount of servings: 1-2 servings (depending on the size of the dog)

Suitable for: Adult dogs, senior dogs

Peanut Butter and Banana

Ingredients:

1 ripe banana

2 tablespoons of creamy peanut butter

1/4 cup rolled oats.

Instructions:

Mash the banana in a bowl, add the peanut butter and oats and mix well.

Place the mixture's little balls on a baking sheet after rolling them into them.

For 15-20 minutes, bake at 350 degrees Fahrenheit.

Calories: approximately 50-70 calories per serving.

Amount of servings: depends on the size of the balls (around 20-30 small balls)

Suitable for: Adult dogs, senior dogs

Sweet Potato and Chicken

Ingredients:

1/2 cup cooked

Mashed sweet potato

1/2 cup cooked, shredded chicken

1/4 cup rolled oats.

Instructions:

Mix all ingredients in a bowl.

Place the mixture's little balls on a baking sheet after rolling them into them.

For 15-20 minutes, bake at 350 degrees Fahrenheit.

Calories: approximately 100-150 calories per serving.

Amount of servings: depends on the size of the balls

(around 20-30 small balls)

Suitable for: Adult dogs, puppies

Apple and Oat Muffins:

Ingredients:

1/2 cup rolled oats

1/4 cup whole wheat flour

1/4 cup unsweetened applesauce

1 egg.

Instructions:

Mix all ingredients in a bowl.

Spoon the mixture into a muffin tin.

Bake at 350 degrees Fahrenheit for 20-25 minutes.

Calories: approximately 50-70 calories per serving.

Amount of servings: 6-8 muffins (depending on the size of the muffins)

Suitable for: Adult dogs, senior dogs

Turkey and Rice Breakfast Bowl:

Ingredients:

1/2 cup cooked, shredded turkey

1/2 cup cooked, white rice

1/4 cup diced vegetables (carrots, green beans, and broccoli)

Instructions:

Mix all ingredients in a bowl. Serve warm.

Calories: approximately 200-250 calories per serving.

Amount of servings: 1-2 servings (depending on the size of the dog)

Suitable for: Adult dogs, senior dogs, working dogs

Berry and Yogurt Parfait:

Ingredients:

1/2 cup plain Greek yogurt

1/4 cup mixed berries (strawberries, blueberries, raspberries)

1/4 cup crushed dog-friendly granola

Instructions:

Layer the yogurt, berries, and granola in a bowl or jar.

Serve chilled.

Calories: approximately 150-200 calories per serving.

Amount of servings: 1-2 servings (depending on the size of the dog)

Suitable for: Adult dogs, senior dogs

Carrot and Chicken Porridge:

Ingredients:

1/2 cup cooked, shredded chicken

1/2 cup cooked, grated carrots

1/4 cup rolled oats

Instructions:

Mix all ingredients in a pot and cook over low heat until thickened.

Serve warm.

Calories: approximately 200-250 calories per serving.

Amount of servings: 1-2 servings (depending on the size of the dog)

Suitable for: Adult dogs, senior dogs, puppies

Pumpkin and Oat:

Ingredients:

1 cup whole wheat flour

1/2 cup rolled oats

1/2 cup canned pumpkin

1 egg

Instructions:

Mix all ingredients in a bowl.

Roll the dough out and cut it into small shapes.

Place the biscuits on a baking sheet and bake at 350 degrees Fahrenheit for 20-25 minutes.

Calories: approximately 50-70 calories per serving.

Amount of servings: depends on the size of the biscuits (around 20-30 small biscuits)

Suitable for: Adult dogs, senior dogs

Beef and Rice Breakfast Bowl:

Ingredients:

1/2 cup cooked, shredded beef

1/2 cup cooked, white rice

1/4 cup diced vegetables (carrots, green beans, and broccoli)

Instructions:

Mix all ingredients in a bowl. Serve warm.

Calories: approximately 250-300 calories per serving.

Amount of servings: 1-2 servings (depending on the

size of the dog)

Suitable for: Adult dogs, senior dogs, working dogs

Salmon and Sweet Potato Treats:

Ingredients:

1/2 cup cooked, mashed sweet potato

1/2 cup cooked, flaked salmon

1/4 cup rolled oats

Instructions:

Mix all ingredients in a bowl.

Place the mixture's little balls on a baking sheet after rolling them into them.

For 15-20 minutes, bake at 350 degrees Fahrenheit.

Calories: approximately 100-150 calories per serving.

Amount of servings: depends on the size of the balls (around 20-30 small balls)

Suitable for: Adult dogs, senior dogs, puppies

Chicken and Rice Casserole:

Ingredients:

1/2 cup cooked, shredded chicken

1/2 cup cooked white rice

1/4 cup diced vegetables (carrots, green beans, and broccoli)

1/4 cup chicken broth.

Instructions:

Mix all ingredients in a casserole dish.

For 20–25 minutes, bake at 350 degrees Fahrenheit.

Calories: approximately 200-250 calories per serving.

Amount of servings: 1-2 servings (depending on the size of the dog)

Suitable for: Adult dogs, senior dogs, working dogs

Turkey and Vegetable Stew:

Ingredients:

1/2 cup cooked, shredded turkey

1/2 cup diced vegetables (carrots, green beans, broccoli, and sweet potato)

1/4 cup chicken broth.

Instructions:

Mix all ingredients in a pot and simmer for 20 minutes.

Serve warm.

Calories: approximately 200-250 calories per serving.

Amount of servings: 1-2 servings (depending on the size of the dog)

Suitable for: Adult dogs, senior dogs, working dogs

Beef and Vegetable Skewers:

Ingredients:

1/2 cup cooked, diced beef

1/2 cup diced vegetables (carrots, green beans, and broccoli)

1 tablespoon olive oil.

Instructions:

Thread the beef and vegetables onto skewers

Brush with olive oil and grill for 8-10 minutes.

Calories: approximately 200-250 calories per serving.

Amount of servings: 1-2 servings (depending on the size of the skewers)

Suitable for: Adult dogs, senior dogs, working dogs

Pork and Sweet Potato Mash:

Ingredients:

1/2 cup cooked, shredded pork

1/2 cup cooked, mashed sweet potato

1/4 cup chicken broth.

Instructions:

Mix all ingredients in a pot and simmer for 15 minutes.

Serve warm.

Calories: approximately 200-250 calories per serving.

Amount of servings: 1-2 servings (depending on the size of the dog)

Suitable for: Adult dogs, senior dogs, working dogs

Fish and Vegetable Bake:

Ingredients:

1/2 cup cooked, flaked fish

1/2 cup diced vegetables (carrots, green beans, broccoli),

1/4 cup chicken broth.

Instructions:

Mix all ingredients in a baking dish.

For 20–25 minutes, bake at 350 degrees Fahrenheit.

Calories: approximately 200-250 calories per serving.

Amount of servings: 1-2 servings (depending on the

size of the dog)

Suitable for: Adult dogs, senior dogs

Lamb and Vegetable Stew:

Ingredients:

1/2 cup cooked, diced lamb

1/2 cup diced vegetables (carrots, green beans, broccoli, and sweet potato)

1/4 cup chicken broth.

Instructions:

Mix all ingredients in a pot and simmer for 20 minutes.

Serve warm.

Calories: approximately 250-300 calories per serving.

Amount of servings: 1-2 servings (depending on the size of the dog)

Suitable for: Adult dogs, senior dogs, working dogs

Turkey and Vegetable Meatballs:

Ingredients:

1/2 cup ground turkey

1/4 cup diced vegetables (carrots, green beans, broccoli),

1/4 cup rolled oats

1 egg.

Instructions:

Mix all ingredients in a bowl.

Small meatballs made from the mixture should be formed, then put on a baking pan

For 15-20 minutes, bake at 350 degrees Fahrenheit.

Calories: approximately 150-200 calories per serving.

Amount of servings: depends on the size of the meatballs (around 20-30 small meatballs)

Suitable for: Adult dogs, senior dogs

Salmon and Brown Rice Salad:

Ingredients:

1/2 cup cooked, flaked salmon

1/2 cup cooked brown rice

1/4 cup diced vegetables (carrots, green beans, and broccoli)

Instructions:

Mix all ingredients in a bowl.

Serve chilled.

Calories: approximately 200-250 calories per serving.

Amount of servings: 1-2 servings (depending on the size of the dog)

Suitable for: Adult dogs, senior dogs

Beef and Vegetable Soup:

Ingredients:

1/2 cup cooked, diced beef,

1/2 cup diced vegetables (carrots, green beans,

broccoli, sweet potato),

1/4 cup beef broth.

Instructions:

Mix all ingredients in a pot and simmer for 20 minutes.

Serve warm.

Calories: approximately 250-300 calories per serving.

Amount of servings: 1-2 servings (depending on the size of the dog)

Suitable for: Adult dogs, senior dogs, working dogs

Pork and Vegetable Stir Fry:

Ingredients:

1/2 cup cooked, diced pork

1/2 cup diced vegetables (carrots, green beans, broccoli, and sweet potato)

1 tablespoon olive oil.

Instructions:

Heat olive oil in a pan over medium heat, add the diced vegetables, and cook for a few minutes.

Add the pork and stir-fry for an additional 5-7 minutes. Serve warm.

Calories: approximately 250-300 calories per serving.

Amount of servings: 1-2 servings (depending on the size of the dog)

Suitable for: Adult dogs, senior dogs, working dogs

Chicken and Vegetable Casserole:

Ingredients:

1/2 cup cooked, shredded chicken

1/2 cup diced vegetables (carrots, green beans, broccoli),

1/4 cup chicken broth.

Instructions:

Mix all ingredients in a casserole dish.

For 20-25 minutes, bake at 350 degrees Fahrenheit.

Calories: approximately 200-250 calories per serving.

Amount of servings: 1-2 servings (depending on the size of the dog)

Suitable for: Adult dogs, senior dogs, working dogs

Beef and Vegetable Stew:

Ingredients:

1/2 cup cooked, diced beef

1/2 cup diced vegetables (carrots, green beans, broccoli, and sweet potato)

1/4 cup beef broth.

Instructions:

Mix all ingredients in a pot and simmer for 20 minutes.

Serve warm.

Calories: approximately 250-300 calories per serving.

Amount of servings: 1-2 servings (depending on the

size of the dog)

Suitable for: Adult dogs, senior dogs, working dogs

Pork and Vegetable Skewers:

Ingredients:

1/2 cup cooked, diced pork

1/2 cup diced vegetables (carrots, green beans, and broccoli)

1 tablespoon olive oil.

Instructions:

Thread the pork and vegetables onto skewers.

Brush with olive oil and grill for 8-10 minutes.

Calories: approximately 250-300 calories per serving.

Amount of servings: 1-2 servings (depending on the size of the skewers)

Suitable for: Adult dogs, senior dogs, working dogs

Fish and Vegetable Bake:

Ingredients

1/2 cup cooked, flaked fish

1/2 cup diced vegetables (carrots, green beans, broccoli)

1/4 cup fish broth.

Instructions:

Mix all ingredients in a baking dish.

For 20-25 minutes, bake at 350 degrees Fahrenheit.

Calories: approximately 200-250 calories per serving.

Amount of servings: 1-2 servings (depending on the size of the dog)

Suitable for: Adult dogs, senior dogs

Turkey and Vegetable Meatloaf:

Ingredients:

1/2 cup ground turkey

1/4 cup diced vegetables (carrots, green beans,

broccoli)

1/4 cup rolled oats

1 egg.

Instructions:

Mix all ingredients in a bowl.

Form the mixture into a loaf shape and place it in a loaf pan.

Bake at 350 degrees Fahrenheit for 30-35 minutes.

Calories: approximately 150-200 calories per serving.

Amount of servings: 1-2 servings (depending on the size of the dog)

Suitable for: Adult dogs, senior dogs

Lamb and Vegetable Casserole:

Ingredients:

1/2 cup cooked, diced lamb

1/2 cup diced vegetables (carrots, green beans,

broccoli)

1/4 cup lamb broth.

Instructions:

Mix all ingredients in a casserole dish.

For 20-25 minutes, bake at 350 degrees Fahrenheit.

Calories: approximately 250-300 calories per serving.

Amount of servings: 1-2 servings (depending on the size of the dog)

Suitable for: Adult dogs, senior dogs, working dogs

Chicken and Vegetable Meatballs:

Ingredients:

1/2 cup ground chicken

1/4 cup diced vegetables (carrots, green beans, and broccoli)

1/4 cup rolled oats

1 egg.

Instructions:

Mix all ingredients in a bowl.

Small meatballs made from the mixture should be formed, then put on a baking pan.

For 15-20 minutes, bake at 350 degrees Fahrenheit.

Calories: approximately 150-200 calories per serving.

Amount of servings: depends on the size of the meatballs (around 20-30 small meatballs)

Suitable for: Adult dogs, senior dogs

Salmon and Vegetable Stew:

Ingredients:

1/2 cup cooked, flaked salmon

1/2 cup diced vegetables (carrots, green beans, broccoli, and sweet potato)

1/4 cup fish broth.

Instructions:

Mix all ingredients in a pot and simmer for 20 minutes.

Serve warm.

Calories: approximately 200-250 calories per serving.

Amount of servings: 1-2 servings (depending on the size of the dog)

Suitable for: Adult dogs, senior dogs

Pork and Vegetable Stir Fry:

Ingredients:

1/2 cup cooked, diced pork

1/2 cup diced vegetables (carrots, green beans, broccoli, and sweet potato)

1 tablespoon olive oil.

Instructions:

Heat olive oil in a pan over medium heat, add the diced vegetables, and cook for a few minutes.

Add the pork and stir-fry for an additional 5-7 minutes.

Serve warm.

Calories: approximately 250-300 calories per serving.

Amount of servings: 1-2 servings (depending on the size of the dog)

Suitable for: Adult dogs, senior dogs, Working dogs

Beef and Vegetable Soup:

Ingredients:

1/2 cup cooked, diced beef

1/2 cup diced vegetables (carrots, green beans, broccoli, and sweet potato)

1/4 cup beef broth.

Instructions:

Mix all ingredients in a pot and simmer for 20 minutes

Serve warm.

Calories: approximately 250-300 calories per serving.

Amount of servings: 1-2 servings (depending on the

size of the dog)

Suitable for: Adult dogs, senior dogs, working dogs

Beef and Barley Stew:

Ingredients:

1 lb lean beef, cubed

1 cup barley

1/2 cup diced carrots

1/2 cup diced celery

1/2 cup diced onion

2 cups beef broth

1 teaspoon olive oil.

Instructions:

In a large pot, heat olive oil over medium heat.

Add the diced onion, celery, and carrots and sauté for 5 minutes.

Add the beef and cook until browned. Stir in the barley and beef broth and bring to a boil.

Reduce heat to low, cover, and simmer for 45-60 minutes or until the barley is tender. Serve warm.

Calories: approximately 400-450 calories per serving.

Amount of servings: 4-6 servings (depending on the size of the dog)

Suitable for: Adult dogs, senior dogs, working dogs

Chicken and Brown Rice:

Ingredients:

1 lb boneless, skinless chicken breasts

1 cup brown rice

2 cups chicken broth

1/2 cup diced carrots

1/2 cup diced celery

1 teaspoon olive oil.

Instructions:

In a large pot, heat olive oil over medium heat.

Add the diced celery and carrots and sauté for 5 minutes.

Add the chicken and cook until browned. Stir in the brown rice and chicken broth and bring to a boil.

Reduce heat to low, cover, and simmer for 45-60 minutes or until rice is tender. Serve warm.

Calories: approximately 400-450 calories per serving.

Amount of servings: 4-6 servings (depending on the size of the dog)

Suitable for: Adult dogs, senior dogs, working dogs

Lamb and Sweet Potato:

Ingredients:

1 lb ground lamb

1 cup diced sweet potato

1/2 cup diced carrots

1/2 cup diced celery

1 teaspoon olive oil.

Instructions:

In a large pot, heat olive oil over medium heat. Add the diced celery and carrots and sauté for 5 minutes.

Add the ground lamb and cook until browned.

Stir in the sweet potato and 1 cup of water and bring to a boil.

Reduce heat to low, cover, and simmer for 30-45 minutes or until sweet potatoes are tender.

Serve warm.

Calories: approximately 400-450 calories per serving.

Amount of servings: 4-6 servings (depending on the size of the dog)

Suitable for: Adult dogs, senior dogs, working dogs

Salmon and Vegetable Medley:

Ingredients:

1 lb salmon fillet

1 cup diced vegetables (carrots, green beans, and broccoli)

1 teaspoon olive oil.

Instructions:

In a large skillet, heat olive oil over medium heat.

For five minutes, add the diced vegetables and sauté them.

Add the salmon fillet and cook until the fish is cooked through.

Serve warm.

Calories: approximately 400-450 calories per serving.

Amount of servings: 4-6 servings (depending on the size of the dog)

Suitable for: Adult dogs, senior dogs, working dogs

Turkey and Vegetable Casserole:

Ingredients:

1 lb ground turkey

1 cup cooked brown rice

1 cup diced vegetables (carrots, green beans, broccoli)

1 cup turkey broth.

Instructions:

Preheat the oven to 350 degrees Fahrenheit. In a large skillet, cook the ground turkey until browned.

Stir in the diced vegetables and cook for an additional 5 minutes.

Stir in the cooked brown rice and turkey broth.

Transfer the mixture to a casserole dish and bake for 30-40 minutes.

Serve warm.

Calories: approximately 400-450 calories per serving.

Amount of servings: 4-6 servings (depending on the size of the dog)

Suitable for: Adult dogs, senior dogs, working dogs

Pork and Vegetable Stir Fry:

Ingredients:

1 lb pork tenderloin

1 cup diced vegetables (carrots, bell peppers, broccoli)

1 teaspoon olive oil

1 teaspoon soy sauce.

Instructions:

In a large skillet, heat olive oil over medium heat.

Cut the pork tenderloin into small strips and add it to the skillet, cook until browned.

For five minutes, add the diced vegetables and sauté them.

Stir in the soy sauce and cook for an additional 2-3 minutes.

Serve warm.

Calories: approximately 400-450 calories per serving.

Amount of servings: 4-6 servings (depending on the size of the dog)

Suitable for: Adult dogs, senior dogs, working dogs

Egg and Vegetable Scramble:

Ingredients:

4 eggs

1/2 cup diced vegetables (spinach, bell peppers, mushrooms)

1 teaspoon olive oil.

Instructions:

Heat olive oil over medium intensity in a large pan.

For two to three minutes, add the diced vegetables

and sauté them.

Crack the eggs into the skillet and scramble until cooked through.

Serve warm.

Calories: approximately 150-200 calories per serving.

Amount of servings: 4-6 servings (depending on the size of the dog)

Turkey and Lentil Stew:

Ingredients:

1 lb ground turkey

1 cup green lentils

1/2 cup diced carrots

1/2 cup diced celery

1/2 cup diced onion

2 cups turkey broth

1 teaspoon olive oil.

Instructions:

In a large pot, heat olive oil over medium heat.

Add the diced onion, celery, and carrots and sauté for 5 minutes.

Add the ground turkey and cook until browned.

Stir in the lentils and turkey broth and bring to a boil.

Reduce heat to low, cover, and simmer for 45-60 minutes or until lentils are tender. Serve warm.

Calories: approximately 400-450 calories per serving.

Amount of servings: 4-6 servings

Beef and Vegetable Casserole:

Ingredients:

1 lb ground beef

1 cup cooked brown rice

1 cup diced vegetables (carrots, green beans, and broccoli)

1 cup beef broth.

Instructions:

Preheat the oven to 350 degrees Fahrenheit

In a large skillet, cook the ground beef until browned. Stir in the diced vegetables and cook for an additional 5 minutes.

Stir in the cooked brown rice and beef broth.

Transfer the mixture to a casserole dish and bake for 30-40 minutes.

Serve warm.

Calories: approximately 400-450 calories per serving.

Amount of servings: 4-6 servings

Chicken and Quinoa:

Ingredients:

1 lb boneless, skinless chicken breasts

1 cup quinoa

2 cups chicken broth

1/2 cup diced carrots

1/2 cup diced celery

1 teaspoon olive oil.

Instructions:

In a large pot, heat olive oil over medium heat.

Add the diced celery and carrots and sauté for 5 minutes.

Add the chicken and cook until browned. Stir in the quinoa and chicken broth and bring to a boil.

Reduce heat to low, cover, and simmer for 20-25 minutes or until quinoa is tender.

 Serve warm.

Calories: approximately 400-450 calories per serving.

Amount of servings: 4-6 servings

Chapter 5

Treats

Peanut Butter and Banana Treats:

Ingredients:

1 cup whole wheat flour

1/2 cup mashed banana

1/2 cup peanut butter

1 egg.

Instructions:

Mix all ingredients in a bowl. Carry the batter out and cut it into little shapes.

Place the treats on a baking sheet and bake at 350 degrees Fahrenheit for 20-25 minutes.

Calories: approximately 50-70 calories per serving.

Amount of servings: depends on the size of the treats (around 20-30 small treats)

Suitable for: Adult dogs, senior dogs

Pumpkin and Oat Treats:

Ingredients:

1 cup whole wheat flour

1/2 cup canned pumpkin

1/2 cup rolled oats.

Instructions:

Mix all ingredients in a bowl.

Carry the batter out and cut it into little shapes.

Place the treats on a baking sheet and bake at 350 degrees Fahrenheit for 20-25 minutes.

Calories: approximately 50-70 calories per serving.

Amount of servings: depends on the size of the treats (around 20-30 small treats)

Suitable for: Adult dogs, senior dogs, puppies

Sweet Potato and Chicken Treats:

Ingredients:

1 cup whole wheat flour

1/2 cup cooked, mashed sweet potato

1/2 cup cooked, shredded chicken.

Instructions:

Mix all ingredients in a bowl.

Carry the batter out and cut it into little shapes.

Place the treats on a baking sheet and bake at 350 degrees Fahrenheit for 20-25 minutes.

Calories: approximately 50-70 calories per serving.

Amount of servings: depends on the size of the treats (around 20-30 small treats)

Suitable for: Adult dogs, senior dogs, working dogs

Apple and Cinnamon Treats:

Ingredients:

1 cup whole wheat flour

1/2 cup diced apple

1 teaspoon cinnamon.

Instructions:

Mix all ingredients in a bowl. Carry the batter out and cut it into little shapes.

Place the treats on a baking sheet and bake at 350 degrees Fahrenheit for 20-25 minutes.

Calories: approximately 50-70 calories per serving.

Amount of servings: depends on the size of the treats (around 20-30 small treats)

Suitable for: Adult dogs, senior dogs, puppies

Carrot and Ginger Treats:

Ingredients:

1 cup whole wheat flour

1/2 cup grated carrots

1 teaspoon ginger.

Instructions:

Mix all ingredients in a bowl.

Carry the batter out and cut it into little shapes.

Place the treats on a baking sheet and bake at 350 degrees Fahrenheit for 20-25 minutes.

Calories: approximately 50-70 calories per serving.

Amount of servings: depends on the size of the treats (around 20-30 small treats)

Suitable for: Adult dogs, senior dogs, working dogs

Meat and Vegetable Treats:

Ingredients:

1 cup whole wheat flour

1/2 cup cooked, diced meat (chicken, beef, pork)

1/2 cup diced vegetables (carrots, green beans, broccoli).

Instructions:

Mix all ingredients in a bowl. Carry the batter out and cut it into little shapes.

Place the treats on a baking sheet and bake at 350 degrees Fahrenheit for 20-25 minutes.

Calories: approximately 50-70 calories per serving.

Amount of servings: depends on the size of the treats (around 20-30 small treats)

Suitable for: Adult dogs, senior dogs, working dogs

Fish and Potato Treats:

Ingredients:

1 cup whole wheat flour

1/2 cup cooked, flaked fish

1/2 cup cooked, mashed potato.

Instructions:

Mix all ingredients in a bowl.

Carry the batter out and cut it into little shapes.

Place the treats on a baking sheet and bake at 350 degrees Fahrenheit for 20-25 minutes.

Calories: approximately 50-70 calories per serving.

Amount of servings: depends on the size of the treats (around 20-30 small treats)

Suitable for: Adult dogs, senior dogs

Chicken and Rice Treats:

Ingredients:

1 cup whole wheat flour

1/2 cup cooked, shredded chicken

1/2 cup cooked white rice.

Instructions:

Mix all ingredients in a bowl. Carry the batter out and cut it into little shapes.

Place the treats on a baking sheet and bake at 350 degrees Fahrenheit for 20-25 minutes.

Calories: approximately 50-70 calories per serving.

Amount of servings: depends on the size of the treats (around 20-30 small treats)

Suitable for: Adult dogs, senior dogs, working dogs

Beef and Vegetable Treats:

Ingredients:

1 cup whole wheat flour

1/2 cup cooked, diced beef

1/2 cup diced vegetables (carrots, green beans, broccoli).

Instructions:

Mix all ingredients in a bowl. Roll the dough out and cut it into small shapes.

Place the treats on a baking sheet and bake at 350 degrees Fahrenheit for 20-25 minutes.

Calories: approximately 50-70 calories per serving.

Amount of servings: depends on the size of the treats (around 20-30 small treats)

Suitable for: Adult dogs, senior dogs, working dogs

Liver and Vegetable Treats:

Ingredients:

1 cup whole wheat flour

1/2 cup cooked, diced liver

1/2 cup diced vegetables (carrots, green beans, broccoli).

Instructions:

Mix all ingredients in a bowl. Carry the batter out and cut it into little shapes.

Place the treats on a baking sheet and bake at 350 degrees Fahrenheit for 20-25 minutes.

Calories: approximately 50-70 calories per serving.

Amount of servings: depends on the size of the treats (around 20-30 small treats)

Suitable for: Adult dogs, senior dogs, working dogs

Chapter 6

Snacks

Peanut Butter and Banana Dog Biscuits:

Ingredients:

1 cup whole wheat flour

1/2 cup rolled oats

1/4 cup peanut butter

1 mashed banana

1 egg

1/4 cup water.

Instructions:

Preheat the oven to 350 degrees Fahrenheit.

In a large bowl, mix the flour, oats, peanut butter, mashed banana, egg, and water.

Roll out the dough on a floured surface and cut it into

desired shapes (bone-shaped is a popular option).

Place the biscuits on a baking sheet and bake for 20-25 minutes or until golden brown.

Calories: approximately 50-60 calories per serving (depending on the size of the biscuit)

Amount of servings: 15-20 biscuits (depending on the size of the dog)

Suitable for: Adult dogs, senior dogs, puppies

Sweet Potato and Chicken Dog Treats:

Ingredients:

1 cup cooked and mashed sweet potato

1 lb cooked and shredded chicken

1 cup whole wheat flour

1 egg

Instructions:

Preheat the oven to 350 degrees Fahrenheit.

In a large bowl, mix the sweet potato, chicken, flour, and egg.

Roll out the dough on a floured surface and cut it into desired shapes.

Place the treats on a baking sheet and bake for 25-30 minutes or until golden brown.

Calories: approximately 50-60 calories per serving (depending on the size of the treat)

Amount of servings: 15-20 treats (depending on the size of the dog)

Suitable for: Adult dogs, senior dogs, working dogs

Pumpkin and Cinnamon Dog Treats:

Ingredients:

1 cup whole wheat flour

1/2 cup rolled oats

1/2 cup pureed pumpkin

1 teaspoon cinnamon

1 egg

1/4 cup water.

Instructions:

Preheat the oven to 350 degrees Fahrenheit.

In a large bowl, mix the flour, oats, pumpkin, cinnamon, egg, and water.

Roll out the dough on a floured surface and cut it into desired shapes.

Place the treats on a baking sheet and bake for 20-25 minutes or until golden brown.

Calories: approximately 50-60 calories per serving (depending on the size of the treat)

Amount of servings: 15-20 treats (depending on the size of the dog)

Suitable for: Adult dogs, senior dogs, puppies

Chicken Jerky Treats:

Ingredients:

1 lb boneless, skinless chicken breasts

1 teaspoon olive oil

Instructions:

Preheat the oven to 175 degrees Fahrenheit.

Cut the chicken breasts into thin strips and brush them with olive oil.

Place the strips on a baking sheet and bake for 2-3 hours or until the strips are dry and crispy.

Calories: approximately 50-60 calories per serving (depending on the size of the treat)

Amount of servings: 15-20 treats (depending on the size of the dog)

Suitable for: Adult dogs, senior dogs, working dogs

Apple and Oat Dog Treats:

Ingredients:

1 cup whole wheat flour

1/2 cup rolled oats

1/2 cup grated apple

1 egg

1/4 cup water

Instructions:

Preheat the oven to 350 degrees Fahrenheit.

In a large bowl, mix the flour, oats, grated apple, egg, and water.

Roll out the dough on a floured surface and cut it into desired shapes.

Place the treats on a baking sheet and bake for 20-25 minutes or until golden brown.

Calories: approximately 50-60 calories per serving (depending on the size of the treat)

Amount of servings: 15-20 treats (depending on the size of the dog)

Suitable for: Adult dogs, senior dogs, puppies

Carrot and Peanut Butter Dog Treats:

Ingredients:

1 cup whole wheat flour

1/2 cup rolled oats

1/4 cup grated carrot

1/4 cup peanut butter

1 egg

1/4 cup water.

Instructions:

Preheat the oven to 350 degrees Fahrenheit.

In a large bowl, mix the flour, oats, grated carrot, peanut butter, egg, and water.

Roll out the dough on a floured surface and cut it into desired shapes.

Place the treats on a baking sheet and bake for 20-25 minutes or until golden brown.

Calories: approximately 50-60 calories per serving (depending on the size of the treat)

Amount of servings: 15-20 treats (depending on the size of the dog)

Suitable for: Adult dogs, senior dogs, working dogs

Blueberry and Yogurt Dog Treats:

Ingredients:

1 cup whole wheat flour

1/2 cup rolled oats

1/2 cup fresh blueberries

1/4 cup plain yogurt

1 egg

1/4 cup water.

Instructions:

Preheat the oven to 350 degrees Fahrenheit.

In a large bowl, mix the flour, oats, blueberries, yogurt,

egg, and water.

Roll out the dough on a floured surface and cut it into desired shapes.

Place the treats on a baking sheet and bake for 20-25 minutes or until golden brown.

Calories: approximately 50-60 calories per serving (depending on the size of the treat)

Amount of servings: 15-20 treats (depending on the size of the dog)

Suitable for: Adult dogs, senior dogs, puppies

Beef Liver Treats:

Ingredients:

1 lb beef liver

1 teaspoon olive oil

Instructions:

Preheat the oven to 350 degrees Fahrenheit.

Cut the beef liver into small strips and brush with olive oil.

Place the strips on a baking sheet and bake for 20-25 minutes or until crispy.

Calories: approximately 50-60 calories per serving (depending on the size of the treat)

Amount of servings: 15-20 treats (depending on the size of the dog)

Suitable for: Adult dogs, senior dogs, Working dogs

Sweet Potato and Chicken Jerky:

Ingredients:

1 cup sweet potatoes

1 lb chicken breast

1 teaspoon olive oil

1 teaspoon of your dog's favorite spice or herbs (optional)

Instructions:

Preheat the oven to 175 degrees Fahrenheit.

Cut the chicken breast and sweet potatoes into thin strips and brush them with olive oil.

Sprinkle with spices or herbs, if desired.

Place the strips on a baking sheet and bake for 2-3 hours or until dry and crispy.

Calories: approximately 50-60 calories per serving (depending on the size of the treat)

Amount of servings: 15-20 treats (depending on the size of the dog)

Suitable for: Adult dogs, senior dogs, active dogs

Apple and Cinnamon Dog Treats:

Ingredients:

1 cup whole wheat flour

1/2 cup rolled oats

1/2 cup grated apple

1 teaspoon cinnamon

1 egg

1/4 cup water.

Instructions:

Preheat the oven to 350 degrees Fahrenheit.

In a large bowl, mix the flour, oats, grated apple, cinnamon, egg, and water.

Carry out the mixture on a floured surface and cut it into wanted shapes.

Place the treats on a baking sheet and bake for 20-25 minutes or until golden brown.

Calories: approximately 50-60 calories per serving (depending on the size of the treat)

Amount of servings: 15-20 treats (depending on the size of the dog)

Suitable for: Adult dogs, senior dogs, puppies

Chapter 7

Special Diets

Grain-Free Recipes

Grain-Free Turkey and Vegetable Stew:

Ingredients:

1 lb ground turkey

1 cup diced sweet potatoes

1 cup diced carrots

1 cup diced green beans

1/2 cup diced onion

1/2 cup chicken broth

1 teaspoon olive oil

Instructions:

In a huge pot, heat the olive oil over medium intensity.

Add the ground turkey and cook until browned.

Add the diced vegetables, and chicken broth, and bring to a simmer.

Cook for 15-20 minutes or until the vegetables are delicate.

Calories: approximately 300 calories per serving

Amount of servings: 4 servings

Suitable for: Adult dogs, senior dogs

Grain-Free Chicken and Vegetable Casserole:

Ingredients:

1 lb boneless, skinless chicken breasts

1 cup diced sweet potatoes

1 cup diced carrots

1 cup diced green beans

1/2 cup diced onion

1/2 cup chicken broth

1 teaspoon olive oil

Instructions:

Preheat the oven to 350 degrees Fahrenheit. In a big pot, heat the olive oil over medium intensity.

Add the chicken breast and cook until golden brown.

Add the diced vegetables, and chicken broth, and bring to a simmer.

Transfer the mixture to a casserole dish and bake for 30-35 minutes or until the vegetables are tender and the chicken is cooked through.

Calories: approximately 300 calories per serving

Amount of servings: 4 servings

Suitable for: Adult dogs, senior dogs

Grain-Free Beef and Vegetable Soup:

Ingredients:

1 lb ground beef

1 cup diced sweet potatoes

1 cup diced carrots

1 cup diced green beans

1/2 cup diced onion

1/2 cup beef broth

1 teaspoon olive oil

Instructions:

In a huge pot, heat the olive oil over medium intensity. Add the ground beef and cook until browned.

Add the diced vegetables, and beef broth, and bring to a simmer.

Cook for 15-20 minutes or until the vegetables are delicate.

Calories: approximately 300 calories per serving

Amount of servings: 4 servings

Suitable for: Adult dogs, senior dogs

Grain-Free Salmon and Vegetable Bake:

Ingredients:

1 lb salmon fillet

1 cup diced sweet potatoes

1 cup diced carrots

1 cup diced green beans

1/2 cup diced onion

1/2 cup chicken broth

1 teaspoon olive oil

Instructions:

Preheat the oven to 350 degrees Fahrenheit.

In a huge pot, heat the olive oil over medium intensity.

Add the diced vegetables, and chicken broth, and bring to a simmer.

Place the salmon fillet in a baking dish and top it with the vegetable mixture.

Bake for 20-25 minutes or until the vegetables are

soft and the salmon is cooked through.

Calories: approximately 300 calories

Calories: approximately 300 calories per serving

Amount of servings: 4 servings

Suitable for: Adult dogs, senior dogs, active dogs

Grain-Free Pork and Vegetable Stir-Fry:

Ingredients:

1 lb pork tenderloin

1 cup diced sweet potatoes

1 cup diced carrots

1 cup diced green beans

1/2 cup diced onion

1/2 cup chicken broth

1 teaspoon olive oil

Instructions:

In a huge pot, heat the olive oil over medium-high intensity.

Add the pork tenderloin and cook until browned.

Remove the pork from the pan and set aside. In the same pan, add the diced vegetables and chicken broth.

Cook for 5-7 minutes or until the vegetables are tender.

Add the pork back to the pan and stir-fry for 2-3 minutes or until the pork is cooked through.

Calories: approximately 300 calories per serving

Amount of servings: 4 servings

Suitable for: Adult dogs, senior dogs, active dogs

Grain-Free Lamb and Vegetable Casserole:

Ingredients:

1 lb ground lamb

1 cup diced sweet potatoes

1 cup diced carrots

1 cup diced green beans

1/2 cup diced onion

1/2 cup chicken broth

1 teaspoon olive oil

Instructions:

Preheat the oven to 350 degrees Fahrenheit.

In a huge pot, heat the olive oil over medium intensity. Add the ground lamb and cook until golden brown.

Add the diced vegetables, and chicken broth, and bring to a simmer.

Transfer the mixture to a casserole dish and bake for 30-35 minutes or until the vegetables are tender and the lamb is cooked through.

Calories: approximately 300 calories per serving

Amount of servings: 4 servings

Suitable for: Adult dogs, senior dogs

Raw Food

Raw Beef and Vegetable Salad:

Ingredients:

1 lb ground beef

1 cup diced carrots

1 cup diced green beans

1/2 cup diced onion

1/2 cup diced celery

1/4 cup olive oil

1 teaspoon lemon juice

Instructions:

In a large bowl, combine the ground beef, diced vegetables, olive oil, and lemon juice.

Mix well and serve immediately.

Calories: approximately 400 calories per serving

Amount of servings: 4 servings

Suitable for: Adult dogs, active dogs

Raw Chicken and Fruit Salad:

Ingredients:

1 lb boneless, skinless chicken breast

1 cup diced apples

1 cup diced pears

1/2 cup diced banana

1/4 cup diced blueberries

1 teaspoon lemon juice

Instructions:

In a large bowl, combine the diced chicken, fruits, and lemon juice.

Mix well and serve immediately.

Calories: approximately 300 calories per serving

Amount of servings: 4 servings

Suitable for: Adult dogs, senior dogs

Raw Pork and Vegetable Skewers:

Ingredients:

1 lb pork tenderloin

1 cup diced sweet potatoes

1 cup diced carrots

1/2 cup diced onion

1/4 cup olive oil

1 teaspoon rosemary

Instructions:

Cut the pork tenderloin and vegetables into bite-size chunks.

Thread the pork and vegetables onto skewers.

In a small bowl, mix the olive oil and rosemary.

Brush the skewers with the mixture and serve.

Calories: approximately 400 calories per serving

Amount of servings: 4 servings

Suitable for: Adult dogs, active dogs

Raw Lamb and Vegetable Patties:

Ingredients:

1 lb ground lamb

1 cup diced sweet potatoes

1 cup diced carrots

1/2 cup diced onion

1/4 cup diced parsley

1 teaspoon rosemary

Instructions:

In a large bowl, combine the ground lamb, diced

vegetables, parsley, and rosemary.

Mix well. Form the mixture into patties and serve.

Calories: approximately 400 calories per serving

Amount of servings: 4 servings

Suitable for: Adult dogs, active dogs

Raw Turkey and Vegetable Meatballs:

Ingredients:

1 lb ground turkey

1 cup diced sweet potatoes

1 cup diced carrots

1/2 cup diced onion

1/4 cup diced parsley

1 teaspoon rosemary

Instructions:

In a large bowl, combine the ground turkey, diced

vegetables, parsley, and rosemary.

Mix well. Form the mixture into meatballs and serve.

Calories: approximately 400 calories per serving

Amount of servings: 4 servings

Suitable for: Adult dogs, active dogs

Raw Salmon and Vegetable Bites:

Ingredients:

1 lb salmon fillet

1 cup diced sweet potatoes

1 cup diced carrots

1/2 cup diced onion

1/4 cup diced parsley

1 teaspoon dill

Instructions:

Cut the salmon fillet and vegetables into bite-size

chunks.

In a small bowl, mix the parsley and dill.

Toss the salmon and vegetables with the herb mixture and serve.

Calories: approximately 400 calories per serving

Amount of servings: 4 servings

Suitable for: Adult dogs, active dogs

Chapter 8

Storage and Serving of Homemade Dog Food

Storing Homemade Dog Food

Storing homemade dog food properly is important to ensure that it stays fresh and safe for your dog to eat. Here are a few tips for storing homemade dog food:

1. Use airtight containers: Use containers that seal tightly to keep the food fresh and prevent any contamination. Glass or plastic compartments with tight-fitting covers function admirably.

2. Store in the refrigerator or freezer: Homemade dog food should be stored in the refrigerator or freezer to prevent bacteria growth. If stored in the refrigerator, it should be consumed within 3 -5 days. If stored in the freezer, it can be kept for up to 6 months.

3. Label and date the food: Label the containers with the type of food and the date it was made to keep track of when it was made and when it needs to be consumed.

4. Portion control: Portion the food into the appropriate serving sizes for your dog, so that you can thaw only what you need for each meal.

5. Thawing the food: When thawing frozen dog food, it should be done in the refrigerator, not at room temperature. This will prevent bacteria growth.

6. Reheat the food: Homemade dog food should be reheated to at least 165°F before serving to kill any bacteria that may have developed during storage.

By following these tips, you can ensure that your dog's homemade food stays fresh and safe for them to consume.

Serving Homemade Dog Food

Serving homemade dog food can be a great way to ensure that your dog is getting a well-balanced and nutritious diet. Here are a few tips for serving homemade dog food:

- Serve at room temperature: Homemade dog food should be served at room temperature, not straight out of the refrigerator or freezer. This will make it more palatable and easier for your dog to eat.

- Use appropriate serving size: Make sure to portion the food into the appropriate serving size for your dog, based on their size, age, and activity level. Consult with your veterinarian for specific recommendations.

- Mix with kibble (if desired): If your dog is used to eating kibble, you can mix the homemade food with their regular kibble to help them transition to the new food

- Monitor their food intake: Observe your dog's food intake, if they don't eat or lose interest in the food, it could be the recipe or ingredients you are using are not suitable for them.

- Keep it varied: Rotate the recipes you use to prepare the homemade dog food, this way you can ensure that your dog is getting a variety of nutrients and it will also prevent them from getting bored with the same food.

- Gradual transition: Gradually introduce the homemade food into your dog's diet over a period of 7-10 days. This will give your dog's digestive system time to adjust and prevent any stomach upset.

- Consult with a vet: If you have any concerns or questions about serving homemade dog food, consult with your veterinarian to make sure that you are meeting your dog's nutritional needs.

By following these tips, you can ensure that your dog is getting the proper nutrition from the homemade food you serve them.

Chapter 9

Health and Wellness

Tips for maintaining a healthy dog

1. Feed a well-balanced diet: Feeding your dog a well-balanced diet that is appropriate for their size, age, and activity level is crucial for maintaining their overall health. This can include a combination of commercial dog food and homemade meals, as well as healthy treats.

2. Regular exercise: Regular exercise is important for maintaining your dog's physical and mental health. This can include walks, runs, playing fetch, and other activities that are appropriate for your dog's breed and age.

3. Regular vet check-ups: Regular vet check-ups are essential for maintaining your dog's health. This includes vaccinations, regular check-ups, and screenings for potential health issues.

4. Preventive care: Preventive care such as regular grooming, dental care, and parasite control can help keep your dog healthy and prevent serious health issues.

5. Training and socialization: Training and socialization can help prevent behavioral issues and improve your dog's overall well-being.

6. Provide mental stimulation: Provide your dog with mental stimulation through interactive toys, puzzle feeders, and training activities to keep their minds active and prevent boredom.

7. Maintaining a clean environment: Keep your dog's environment clean by regularly cleaning their bedding, food and water bowls, and living areas.

8. Monitor for signs of illness: Be aware of your dog's behavior and physical condition, and monitor for any signs of illness or discomfort. If you notice any changes, contact your

veterinarian for advice.

9. Provide proper hydration: Proper hydration is essential for your dog's health. Make sure to always have fresh, clean water available for your dog to drink.

10. Proper identification: Proper identification such as a collar with a tag or a microchip is essential in case your dog gets lost or separated from you.

By following these tips, you can help ensure that your dog is healthy and happy. Remember to always consult with a veterinarian for any specific concerns about your dog's health.

Common Diseases in Dogs and How To Treat Them Naturally

- Arthritis: Arthritis is a common health issue in older dogs and can cause pain and stiffness in their joints. Natural remedies for arthritis include glucosamine and chondroitin supplements, omega-3 fatty acids, and turmeric.

- Digestive issues: Dogs can suffer from various digestive issues such as vomiting, diarrhea, and constipation. Natural remedies for digestive issues include probiotics, ginger, and peppermint.

- Anxiety and stress: Dogs can experience anxiety and stress due to various reasons such as loud noises, travel, or changes in their environment. Natural remedies for anxiety and stress include calming pheromones, herbal supplements such as chamomile or valerian root, and aromatherapy using essential oils.

- Allergies: Dogs can develop allergies to certain foods, environmental factors, or even to certain types of flea or tick treatments. Natural remedies for allergies include omega-3 fatty acids, antioxidants, and herbal supplements such as quercetin and bromelain.

- Skin issues: Dogs can suffer from various skin issues such as itching, hot spots, and dry skin. Natural remedies for skin issues include coconut oil, aloe vera, and omega-3 fatty acids.

- Ear infections: Dogs are prone to ear infections due to their ear shape and the accumulation of wax and debris. Natural remedies for ear infections include ear-cleaning solutions, tea tree oil, and garlic.

- UTI: Urinary tract infections are common health issues in dogs and can be caused by various factors. Natural remedies for UTI include cranberry supplements, d-mannose, and probiotics.

- Dental issues: Dental issues such as tartar buildup, gum disease, and bad breath are common in dogs. Natural remedies for dental issues include dental chews, coconut oil, and parsley.

- Fleas and Ticks: Fleas and ticks can cause

itching and skin irritation in dogs. Natural remedies for fleas and ticks include neem oil, citrus, and rosemary.

Please note that it is important to consult with a veterinarian before using any natural remedies as some remedies may be harmful to some dogs depending on their health condition or the medications they are taking.

Conclusion

Tips for transitioning to homemade dog food

1. Gradual transition: Gradually transitioning your dog to homemade food is important to avoid any stomach upset or other health issues. Start by mixing a small amount of homemade food with their current food and gradually increase the amount over a period of a week or two.

2. Monitor your dog's response: Keep an eye on your dog's response to the new food. If they seem to be having any stomach upset, diarrhea, or vomiting, stop the transition and consult with a veterinarian.

3. Keep variety: Mixing up the ingredients in your homemade dog food can help prevent boredom and keep your dog interested in its food.

4. Consult with a veterinarian: Consult with a veterinarian to ensure that the homemade dog

food you are preparing is nutritionally balanced and appropriate for your dog's size, age, and health condition.

5. Use a balanced recipe: Use a balanced recipe that includes all the necessary nutrients such as protein, carbohydrates, fats, vitamins, and minerals.

6. Proper portion control: It's important to monitor the amount of food you give to your dog to avoid overfeeding, which can lead to weight gain and other health issues.

7. Keep track of your dog's health: Keep track of your dog's weight, energy levels, and overall health during the transition period.

8. Be consistent: Once you have transitioned your dog to homemade food, it's important to stick to a consistent diet to maintain their health.

9. Store properly: Homemade dog food should be stored in the refrigerator or freezer to prevent spoilage and bacteria growth.

10. Keep it fresh: Homemade dog food should be made fresh and should not be stored for long periods of time.

Transitioning to homemade dog food can take some time and patience, but with proper planning and monitoring, you can ensure that your dog is getting the best possible nutrition. Remember to always consult with a veterinarian if you have any concerns about your dog's health or diet.

In conclusion, a homemade dog recipes cookbook can be a valuable resource for dog owners who want to provide their furry friends with nutritious, healthy, and delicious meals. These recipes can be tailored to meet the specific dietary needs of dogs with allergies, and can also be adjusted to suit personal preferences.

However, it's important to remember that these homemade recipes should not be used as a complete and balanced diet for your dog and it's always a good idea to consult with a veterinarian before making any significant changes to your dog's diet.

Additionally, it is important to use only fresh, whole ingredients and avoid any ingredients that may be harmful to dogs. The cookbook should include instructions, ingredients, and any important notes for the recipes. By following these guidelines, you can create a cookbook that will not only provide your dog with delicious and healthy meals but also give you peace of mind knowing that you are providing your dog with the best nutrition possible.

Printed in Great Britain
by Amazon